The Church of Women

Stephanie Steiner

Copyright © 2022 Stephanie Steiner

All rights reserved.

for Amaka

Your existence is a divine gift.
I feel blessed to be your Mother.
May my lines inspire you to continue to follow your path
unapologetically and in tune with your inner wisdom.

for my Mother

Your strength is my teacher.
Your power is my inspiration.
You are the woman I adore the most.

for my Grandmothers

I feel your presence in spirit.
I feel your protection and guidance.
My gratitude and love for you are infinite.

for all Women of the present and the past

You are the reason I share my gift.
I encourage you to explore and embrace your very own
journey towards your soul.
Despite whatever may be around and outside of you -
hang on to the love you carry within. It is your guide
towards your joy, your happiness, and your purpose.

This book is more than a dream or desire coming true - it is a testimony and a manifesto for all women. While sharing my personal story, I tell the stories of millions of women who might not have the chance or the courage to give their pain and joy of being a woman a voice.

You can come to the Church of Women at any point in time.
You don't need to prepare yourself for it.
You are more than ready.
You don't need to do anything to take part.
You already belong.
You have a seat at the table for life and beyond because you are part of a gigantic family of women worldwide.
Your existence is a unique gift.
Never forget this!

Shungo - from my heart to yours,

                                                      Stephanie Steiner

contents

shadows..9

transformation................................37

the source.......................................59

shadows

The Church of Women

Stephanie Steiner

what they told me

you are too much
you are too demanding
you are not good enough
you are too emotional
you are too dramatic
you are too sensitive
you are so frustrated
you are so unhappy
you are not a good mother
you are not a good wife
you are the reason he left you
you're thinking too much
you're always complaining
you should chill
you should shave your armpits
you should be quiet
you should wear heels
you should let your hair grow
you should behave
you should smile more
you should stop being childish
you should wear less make-up
you should dress your age
you should color your hair
you should stop wearing tight pants
you should stop wearing short skirts
you should get a boob job
your body's out of shape
you look sick
you look tired

The Church of Women

Stephanie Steiner

I internalized voices from outside
I internalized the harsh words of judgment
I internalized the cruel opinions of strangers
I internalized the helpful advice of loved ones

what they told me shaped my thoughts
what they told me shaped my opinions
what they told me shaped my beliefs
what they told me shaped my internal monologue

that's when the unity within got disrupted
that's when the conflict within erupted
that's when the internal war started

I started to become my worst enemy
I started to stop listening to the loving voice within
I started to doubt myself
I started to tell myself lies
I started to believe the lies they told me
I started to be unable to connect to my inner truth
I started to forget the truth
I started to believe I was unworthy of being loved
I started to disconnect from my love for myself

The Church of Women

Stephanie Steiner

txt wallpaper

my text messages resemble novels
breaking down my psyche and my emotional state
I put my heart into this
but clearly, he doesn't see the art in it
because his response is
too many words build up confusion

I am blinded by the lies in my mind
that blamed me
instead of realizing that
he is too simple-minded
and simply can't decipher me

The Church of Women

Stephanie Steiner

emotional catastrophes

your eyes want to kill my confidence
my highs want to love your absence
but the craving for emotional catastrophes
outweighs the presence of clarity
I am obsessed with you and your insanity
I am a junkie for your madness
I despise and love your badass
your soul is as dark as the night
and mine shines too bright
shines too light
maybe this explains
why we fight and fight and fight
our love is like a wall with too many cracks
too many holes
you don't love me
but you fuck all of them hoes
I suppose I gotta move on
but the beat keeps dropping
I can't move on

The Church of Women

Stephanie Steiner

my
inner
team
is
at war

The Church of Women

Stephanie Steiner

I drowned myself
thinking that
doing something
is the only solution
to my confusion

The Church of Women

I change my opinions
like bed sheets

Stephanie Steiner

I am torn
between
opinions
that all make sense

The Church of Women

thanks to daddy
I am drawn to losers

Stephanie Steiner

he called my poetry
nursery rhymes
and left me feeling
like my dad finally
found the voice
to speak to me

The Church of Women

I allowed him
to destroy me
so I could
finally
build me up
from scratch again

Stephanie Steiner

I denied myself
so he would
love me

The Church of Women

what should I do
became my desperate way of
asking
can you still love me
when I am lost

Stephanie Steiner

I lost myself
recreating the drama
I tried to escape

The Church of Women

I lost my love
paying his bills
trying to prove
I am worthy of being
loved

Stephanie Steiner

I lost myself
telling my Mother
that I can be the version
of herself
she failed to become

The Church of Women

I hated my DNA
for not making me look
like one of Heidi's girls

Stephanie Steiner

how many more times
do I have to recreate my drama
before I take the time to solve it?

The Church of Women

how many more times
do I have to talk about my pain
before I dare to feel it?

Stephanie Steiner

how many more liars
do I have to meet to
finally, uncover
my lies?

The Church of Women

transformation

The Church of Women

Stephanie Steiner

transformation is a process
thought by thought
moment by moment
new patterns manifest new forms
it takes time for a butterfly
to spread its wings

- the art of being patient in an ocean
full of resolutions-

The Church of Women

writing
has
saved
me
from
killing
myself

Stephanie Steiner

writing has saved me from killing myself

I went to the pain cave
without my wolf pack
I must have lost them along the road

I encountered my demons in the streets of London
unprotected and vulnerable
as a flower on a concrete floor
threatened to be destroyed any second

they took me, hostage, for quite a while
I lost track of time

I went to the pain cave
with a pen and paper
I wrote them a letter and told them
you can do your worst to me
because

writing has saved me from killing myself
and I won't allow
the shadows of a painful past
long gone
to take away
the present of my presence
in the infinite preciousness
of the now

The Church of Women

Stephanie Steiner

for you
love is just a theory
with no concept of reality
you dream of success and family
but you're not able to contribute responsibility
you show me nothing but mental instability
while pretending to be connected to a source of ancient spirituality
you create an image of soulful sexuality
while in reality
you practice a dangerous kind of sexual liberty
you are the ultimate prick to me
a soulful brother wanna-be
I see you
you can't lie to me

The Church of Women

Stephanie Steiner

in another dimension
you are a perfect match
but in this one
you are hard to catch

your spirit is close to mine
but when I leave your presence
it continues to travel
through space and time

I dream of us like a mad woman
but realize you will never be mine

and though I am unique to you
I'll never be the one for you too

as harsh as it sounds and
as sad as it seems
pain is my constant reminder
to forget you, us,
and all my silly little love story dreams

if this was love
I don't want a single piece
and baby, if I keep chasing you
I will never find peace

The Church of Women

Stephanie Steiner

am I too much
or
are you just not
man enough?

The Church of Women

Stephanie Steiner

what I told my Self

I admire my confidence
I admire how bold I am
I admire my persistence
I admire how connected I am to my emotions
I admire my vibrancy
I admire how empathetic I am
I admire my honesty
I admire how I allow my feelings to flow freely
I admire how I juggle all these different roles
I admire how I create healthy boundaries
I admire my independence
I admire my analytical abilities
I admire how I verbalize my opinion
I admire the fire I have inside
I admire how confident I am about my body
I admire how well I express myself
I admire how I developed my distinct style
I admire my confidence to wear my hair short
I admire my confidence to be unapologetic
I admire that I never cover my feelings
I admire how connected I am to my inner child
I admire my confidence to stand out
I admire my confidence to wear what I want
I admire my confidence to have silver hair
I admire my confidence to show my curves
I admire my confidence to dress sexy
I admire how much I love my body
I admire my confidence to be natural
I admire how authentic I am
I admire that I never wear a mask
I admire my confidence to age

The Church of Women

I thanked him for his insults
cause they made me grow
thorns of compassion
for my inner demons

Stephanie Steiner

I am worthy
especially when I am struggling
to find a way

The Church of Women

I believe
change
is the
blueprint of
God

Stephanie Steiner

I make peace with the insults
the broken promises
and the idea
his love could
kill my self-hate

The Church of Women

I found myself
at 4 a.m.
when I allowed the pain
to speak to me

Stephanie Steiner

I found myself
realizing
my Mother saw the best in me

The Church of Women

I stopped trying
to impress
others
to make me
feel better
about myself

Stephanie Steiner

I allow my confusion
to be
fighting it
makes it worse

The Church of Women

I am allowed to be loved
especially
when I consider myself
ugly

the source

The Church of Women

Stephanie Steiner

Miss Pompadour

Extravagant and sound
she is strutting around

They call her Miss Pompadour
´cause everywhere she goes
she whispers l'amour

Love is her principle
and laughter her cure
Fabulous, phenomenal Miss Pompadour

She is inside every woman
mysteriously woven into her skin
she feels the unsaid and senses everything

She embraces her divinity
and shines it through every pore
Intuition is her backbone
guiding her in stormy times back to her shore

She is the eternal queen
that lives in every woman's righteous dream

The Church of Women

Stephanie Steiner

the tight grip of
her soft hands
lets the young boy know
where he belongs to
the sweet sound of
her voice
when she sings him
to sleep
lets the small boy know
what care means
growing up
he looks up at her
many times
every time his & her eyes
meet
a burst of warm light
flashes into his heart
and he knows
what love is
long before the word
love has entered his mind

-for a true mother-

The Church of Women

Stephanie Steiner

Manifesto for the Church of Women

I crave a congregation of women
a nation of strong and supportive women
who refuse to handle abuse
as their daily business

mutual empowerment
shall be their daily bread
genuine care for each other
shall be their intention
wealth and health shall be their goals

constant competition
doesn't just kill the vibe
it kills our nurturing wombs
wombs that bring life into this world

endless envy is the
destructive lunch box
we shall stop devouring day by day
and stop feeding each other day by day

instead
appreciation and admiration
for each other
shall infuse
our thoughts and deeds
towards our
beloved sisters

The Church of Women

we shall accept
and furthermore
love our female forms
beautiful and diverse
and stop torturing our minds and bodies
wanting to become less
to blend in
to become more like the women
society celebrates
thin but with a fat ass
fit but not too muscular
rather well-proportioned
simply sexy
like a delicious meal
pleasing to look at
desirable
always available for male pleasure
always ready to satisfy male needs

we need to stop falling for these lies
they keep vaccinating our minds
like we're not enough
or we're just too much
or we're only relevant
when we become less us

we don't need a women's quota
we need a female revolution
we don't need to count the problems
we need to dig into solutions

Stephanie Steiner

we need to believe in our power
and drop all of our confusion
we need to embrace our different roles
and feed into our female revolution

we can't become weak and quiet
submissive and obedient
we can't stop shining our true light
because we are afraid to stand out and be seen

our true power will never be invisible
it will always be a bright, colorful rainbow
that no one can ignore or deny

I crave a congregation of women
a nation of strong and supportive women
who care for each other
and dare to question authority

I crave for us women
to come together and share our stories
full of pain and love
at the same round table
women of all shapes
colors and backgrounds
let us create
a church of women
where we start to celebrate
the divine female power
that resides in
all of us

The Church of Women

Stephanie Steiner

Mother Earth gave birth
to beautiful daughters and sons
the flowers
the trees
the wheatgrass

Mother Earth gave birth
to the strong wombs that
carry and nourish life

The Church of Women

Stephanie Steiner

I struggled to find
my way
and even though
I went astray
the source always brought me
back to the truth

The Church of Women

Stephanie Steiner

they call it resilience
I call it divine grace

The Church of Women

Stephanie Steiner

everything is connected
through one long thread

My Mother

I was born through the strength of a young woman who had to fight hard for recognition in a man's world. I witnessed my Mother's growth through her struggle of being a hard worker and a single mum. She made a lot of sacrifices to reach independence.

My Mother was put down, ridiculed, and envied a lot, even by her own family. She had to prove multiple times that she was strong-willed enough to take over the family business.

As a master stonemason, she taught me that a woman could be just as strong as a man. Growing up, I was taught feminism without any feminist narrative. My Mother broke free from the shackles of a judgemental environment by continuously pursuing her chosen path.

To me, she truly is the embodiment of an emancipated woman.
She fought hard to be able to not ask for permission from a man. She fought hard for her independence as a human being. However, it should be natural to every human being regardless of gender. Regardless of skin color. Regardless of background.

My Mother earned her own money, so not even once did she have to ask a man, "Honey, can I buy this?".

Whether we want to admit it or not, financial independence is the vital key to freedom for most women around the globe.

I'm afraid I have to disagree with people who consider money an unimportant, unnecessary, or even evil factor in independence. To us women, financial stability is the only way to break free from a toxic environment and find and follow our paths.

If you struggle to pay your bills, you will not be able to express yourself freely. Your mind will circle ways to make money to secure your basic needs. So often, you will find yourself in rather unsatisfying situations because you haven't created conditions that allow you the freedom to make better choices for yourself.

Your creativity will not be able to flow, and therefore you will not blossom into the flower that you are.

Only if you reach a state beyond struggle will you be able to elevate, grow and move towards a sound and soulful independent life.

Frequently I have experienced the fear of not making it and not being able to live a comfortable life creating art. But there has been a force inside me - I refer to it as the source - that keeps me going. This force fuels me with an overload of inspiration and motivation to share my art with the world.

This book was only possible because of the vital energy my Mother passed on to me.

Ich liebe Dich, Mama!

My Daughter

A Mother's love can be smooth like a breeze on a hot day and brutal as a heavy storm in fall.
A Mother's love can connect and unite but can cut and destroy if necessary.
A Mother's love knows when to build and knows when to kill.

I didn't know true love until I was blessed to have a child. A child I had dreamt of my whole adolescence. A child - beautiful and bright - that I sometimes can't quite grasp that she came into this world through my womb. Through her, I can see my beauty. Through her, I have found my place and my worth. I have learned to appreciate my body and its vast capability through her.

Being a mother opened a portal to a world I had to navigate without a manual, a map, and a compass. To find the right direction, I had no choice but to trust my intuition in a jungle full of well-intentioned advice from people close (and not so close) to me.

Being a mother makes me look at my existence as one bead in a long continuous thread filled with beads. I finally feel like I belong. It makes me feel important, worthy, and part of the bigger picture.

I admire my daughter for her sharp, clear mind that cannot easily be tainted and manipulated. She can see through things for what they are rather than what they seem at first glance. This ability makes her a mighty warrior in a world full of deceptions.

My daughter is that one person who looks at me with absolute honesty. That honesty is sometimes very shocking but necessary, not to say vital. Without honesty, how can there be change, growth, and transformation?

Being my daughter's Mother has been the catalyst for my transformation. It made me shift my focus from fear to confidence, from despair to hope. I started looking at my shadow, darkness, and weakness and realized that they were far less scary than they seemed. I needed to find love within, even for those unwanted and ugly parts of myself. They screamed for my attention and needed my healing. Because - how can I raise a strong woman if I am not strong myself? How can I teach her self-love if I do not love myself? How can I tell her to follow her dreams if I don't follow mine?

Indeed, one does not need to become a mother to experience all of this. But for me, it was part of my journey, and I am deeply grateful for this experience every day.

My dear Amaka,

I love you!

about the author

Stephanie Steiner is a poet and dancer from Germany.

She was professionally trained in dance in Munich and New York City and studied theatre and film in Vienna. Stephanie appeared on national tv as a judge for the dance show Maltina Dance All and worked as a creative director for product launches and music videos in Nigeria.

For more than 15 years, she has been sharing her love for dance as a dance teacher.

Writing has been Stephanie's companion since her childhood. Her diary became her refuge and her safe space. When she came across poetry and its freedom and versatility of expression, she knew it was the perfect language to speak her mind and express her emotions.

Stephanie is the founder of #poetrymeetsmotion, a performance concept that features poetry in combination with dance.

Her mission is to inspire and empower girls and women worldwide with her art.

Printed in Poland
by Amazon Fulfillment
Poland Sp. z o.o., Wrocław